WHEN I'M WITH MY MOMMY, I MISS DADDY!

By:

Taneka Hamilton

In memory of my baby brother Joseph
April 24, 1988 to July 3, 2020

Dedication

This book is dedicated to my two beautiful children, Tamea and Jakai. Also to every child that doesn't know how to talk about their feeling of living in two different homes. Don't forget you're awesome, special and loved.

Brooke runs to the playground and grabs Ayden's hand. "What are you doing?" Ayden cried.

"Mommy is here! It's Swap weekend," said Brooke.

"Huh!" said Ayden.

"You know we have two houses. Well, Mom and Dad do. Mommy has one, and Daddy has one. On the weekend, Mommy goes to Daddy's house, and Daddy comes to our house so we don't have to go house to house every week," said Brooke.

Brooke spots the brown car in front of the house. "Ayyyyyden, look!" Brooke yelled.

"Yes!" Ayden yelled. "Daddy is here!"

"Mommy, are you leaving? I miss you when I am not in school," said Brooke. "I will be back to take you to school on Monday. I have to work this weekend. Ayden, I'm leaving; come give Mommy kisses. See you later.

I made dinner. Make sure to make airplanes for Ayden to eat his broccoli," said Mommy.

"Mommy made dinner. Let's eat! Yummy chicken and broccoli. That's yucky!" said Ayden.

"I love broccoli; it makes me strong," said Brooke.

"Come on, big boy. Don't you want muscles? Eating your broccoli will give you big muscles like me," said Daddy.

Daddy sprinkles a little muscle magic on the broccoli so Ayden can get muscle. "Daddy, look, he ate it all. OMG! Ayden, you're going to be so strong like Daddy!" Brooke yelled.

"Ayden, Brooke, I have your dinosaur and princess pajamas," said Daddy.

Brooke ran into the kitchen. She fell to the floor. Ayden put his pajamas on and ran behind her.

"Daddy! Daddy! Brooke is sad," said Ayden.

"Come here, Brooke. What's wrong?" said Daddy.

"I miss Mommy. Why can't we all just be in one house all the time!" Brooke cried. "Sometimes Mommy and Daddy need a time out. We love you, and that's what matters most. Mommy will be back on Monday to take you to school.

Put on your pajamas so we can watch a movie and eat popcorn," said Daddy.

The next day was fun!

Ayden was a good boy. He always stayed right under Dad. He carried him all around the house.

Brooke loved to see the two of them play.

When Monday came, their mother was back to take them to school. Brooke was excited. Mom prepared them for school.

Ayden was always asking for Dad.

"But Mommy, Dad was here yesterday," Ayden asked.

They repeated this talk every day.

But Mommy was patient and did not mind. "Sometimes Mommy and Daddy need a break. We love you, and that's what matters most," said Mommy.

"I miss Daddy. Why can't we all just be in one house all the time!" Brooke cried.

"Maybe we can call Daddy to see if he wants to come over for dinner and story before bed," said Mommy.

"Yes!" they yelled.

"Daddy will come to eat dinner and read a story when he gets off of work," said Mommy.

"Daddy!!!!!" said Mom, running to the door.

"Brooke, go set the table for dinner. Ayden, go pick out a bedtime story. Daddy, the kids are having a hard time with two houses.

You drop off at school; I pick up. When you get off of work, come over for dinner and story time before bed."

About the Author

My name is Taneka Hamilton, a 34-year-old Chicago native mother of two. I moved to Los Angeles in 2010. Moving so far away from everything I loved definitely molded me into a woman! My passion has always been children. I never wanted to teach but always wanted to educate. I was always intrigued by the "bad" children, the ones with mischievous behaviors that no one wants to deal with! I volunteered many years at my daughter's elementary school, and I was hands-on with the principal and children. A few years ago, I began teaching pre-kindergarten, and believe me when I tell you that the behavior that starts at three and four years old is a bit much! I have co-parented effectively for the past 15 years. Helping others learn how to co-parent effectively has always been a passion of mine! Co-parenting rehab is the gateway to assist others raise happy healthy children, even when they don't prefer their child's other parent. A child's mental and emotional state is important to grooming a stable adult.

Feel free to follow Taneka on the following social media platforms:

www.Facebook.com/coparentingrehab
www.Instagram.com/co_parentingrehab
www.coparentingrehab.com